Thousands Pass Here Every Day

Mary Smith

Indigo Dreams Publishing

First Edition: Thousands Pass Here Every Day
First published in Great Britain in 2012 by:
Indigo Dreams Publishing
132 Hinckley Road
Stoney Stanton
Leics
LE9 4LN

www.indigodreams.co.uk

ISBN 978-1-907401-91-6

British Library Cataloguing in Publication Data. A CIP record for this book can be obtained from the British Library.

Designed and typeset in Palatino Linotype by Indigo Dreams.
Cover design by Ronnie Goodyer of Indigo Dreams.

Printed and bound in Great Britain by The Russell Press Ltd.
www.russelpress.com on FSC paper and board sourced from sustainable forests.

To Jon and David

Acknowledgements

Two people on the top of my list to thank are poets Tom Pow and Andrew Forster. Tom said he would make me write poems – and he did. Andy introduced me to the terror and joy of reading them to an audience – and taught me the importance of having my reading list prepared and rehearsed. I greatly value the generous support and advice they have given over the years. Other friends and fellow-writers have also provided support: Liz Niven; Chrys Salt whose 'Tupperware Bowl of Fate' at the Bakehouse gave me the opportunity to try out new work and everyone in the Dumfries Writers' Group.

Thanks to Ronnie and Dawn of Indigo Dreams for having faith in this collection and for Dawn's determination that the preparation of the manuscript should be 'pleasure not pressure'.

Some of the poems in this collection have been previously published in *Poetry Scotland*; *Lallans*; *Southlight*; *Nomad*; *Second Light* (now *Artemis*); *Markings*; *The Herald*; *Earth Heritage* and, in German translation, *Tarentelle Magazine of the Werkkreiss Literatur der Arbeitswelt.*

Poems have also appeared in two poetry pamphlets: *Voices from Glentrool & Merrick* and *The Big Hill* and in anthologies: *Outside of a Dog* (Chroma, 2000) *My Mother Threw Knives* (Second Light Publication, 2006); and *Glasgow's Hidden City* 1 and 5.

CONTENTS

Thousands Pass Here Every Day

Scene shifters

Millions of years in the making
moorland, hill and heather,
mosses and bog.

A continuous chain of actions,
reactions –

earthquakes, volcanoes, glaciers,
ever changing weather
people, planting, felling, farming …

Landscape today is not an end result,
but only a single frame
in a long-running, slow motion movie.

How well will we act our parts
in the next scene?

Hush

No one was here when lands crashed together,
no one to witness volcanic flames erupt
in fevered dance, nor see in hot lava tears,
this landscape's beginnings.

When glaciers scoured rock faces,
carved mountains, opened rivers and lochs,
no one felt the icy touch
of their slow slide to the sea.

Except the wind, which still carries stories
of what once was, and how things came to be.

But the why of it lies deep
beneath its whisper,
in a silence with power
to unlock mysteries.

Graptolites

writing on the rock
stories of ocean life
aeons ago.

Collision

500 million years ago the Iapetus Ocean
began to close – slowly.
400 million years ago England
crashed into Scotland –
a collision which threw up mountains
as high as the Alps, to be ground
down to size by Ice Ages.

Trying to absorb unimaginable time spans
we telescope the years,
give labels to tectonic history:
Ordovician,
Silurian,
Devonian –
stuff of legends.

Cairnsmore's love story

Like lovers who come together
with desperate longing,
tectonic plates collided in orgasms
of crashing waves, turning
world and ocean upside down.

Passions ignited, blood heated
fierce in the veins.
Fires quenched, love cooled,
held fast in an icy grip, blizzards
blind lovers to core-deep truths:

ice moves, smoothes harsh corners;
hearts, toughened, beat stronger.

Ocean

Turned inside out, upside down,
ocean's floor rose into light
sea bed became mountain peak,
rocky crags where peregrines fly
and ravens cry.

A modern malapropism

I'm reading about
oceanic bryophytes –
some very rare, in woodland gorges.

I look up bryophytes:
the dictionary tells me
a member of one of the main groups
of the vegetable kingdom, mosses and
liverworts
and I, misreading,
imagine rows of German sausages
pink and plump, emerging
from the ocean to disport
amongst ancient oaks.

Silver Flowe

Living history charts
centuries of change, decay, re-birth.

Peat bog stirs genetic memories
binds us to ancestors
buried deep.

Stars in a richly textured sky
reflected in dark pools.

Watery world

wavering sunlight
burn water, peat brown
fringes of emerald mosses

ice age scrieving
on rocky slopes,
valleys,
home to rivers.

Elements of the natural world –
rocks, trees, water –
keep us close to the earth,
to mountains, forests, burns
nourish our spirit
as you did for those long gone:
Mesolithic, Neolithic, Bronze Age …

Big Water of Fleet

High above the viaduct, black specks
against brilliant blue,
swifts swoop and swirl, ceaselessly.

Faultless acrobats, they scream delight
at their own mad careening:
hurtle down to skim the river

where gauze-winged dragonflies hover,
jewel bright in the sun, and pebbles gleam
smooth in quiet shallows.

But see, sometimes this river rages,
snarls and snaps,
gulps down huge chunks of bank.

Beneath clear water,
a bush of yellow broom
lies drowned.

Erratic

A'm no keen oan bein cried an 'erratic':
soons as though A staggert here,
stottin fu. Tellin ye, it wisnae me:
a big glacier did it –
an then it meltet away.

A wisnae daein nothin wrang whin
it gied me a shove, wheeched me up,
whirled me aroon lik A wis
nae mair wechtie nor a balloon.
Next meenit, heid ower heels,
breengin doon thon hill.

An erratic is a boulder transported and deposited by a glacier. They are useful indicators of patterns of former ice flow.

Bargrennan Cairn

Stone on stone on stone,
powerful reminder of a people
claiming a right to this land,
symbols of ancestors' rituals, beliefs.

A new cycle of life
kept you here: the need
to care for animals,
plant crops, bury your dead
ended nomadic existence,

changed your relationship with the world;
connected people and landscape,
past and present –
our lives linked to yours.

You could never have guessed,
we'd use your cairns,
your hammer heads and urns
to read our landscape,
learn our past, consider
our future.

Cairnsmore of Fleet

He's a bit of bruiser, a bully of a mountain.
Head in a black cloud, he scatters
ankle-breaking holes on the ground,
wraps his summit in chilly fingers of mist.

Then, in forgiving mood, he lifts the gloom,
shows off the glories of Galloway.

Balancing act

On one side,
a fast growing green death; fish killed
in acid waters, wildlife habitats
destroyed –
paper produced, pallets, packing cases,
employment created.

On the other,
ancient oak woods, centuries old
grow on debris left behind
by glacial streams –
oaks, birch, hazel, rowan,
hawthorn, holly, ash.

Forestry worker

His life, shared with trees,
breaking his back planting –
spade in, pull to the side,
tree in, stamp it down.
Had to do two thousand a day,
no time to stop.

Twenty years later, felling –
saw the trunk, sned the branches
load up, haul them out.
He was the first
to use a chain saw – forefront
of cutting edge technology.

Now, he's retired,
his son-in-law does the job –
sits in a cab
behind a computer screen,
presses keys,
rarely has to touch a tree.

Harvest haiku

Apple drops from tree
Lies quiet in undergrowth
Fine feast for thrushes

Red rowan berries
Bright against darkening sky
Winter's on the way

Brambles cluster thick
In hedgerows, promises of
Crumble and cream

Modern farm methods
Harvest moon gleams bright
On black plastic bales

Cardoness prayer hoose

Cooried in trees' encirclin airms
its grey stane waas abune the craigs
the chaipel ower the shore
gies easefu welcome.

Inby, weans mak it bonnie
wi yella ragweed,
sea daisies, tangle, shells,
stanes painted jewel bricht.

The wun's sough, gulls'
lanesome chirk, the sea's sang,
slowin the warld,
upliftin the hert.

Staunin stanes

We're ainly stanes, gret muckle stanes,
staunin thoosans o years
like ayeways,
daein nocht bit staun,
takkin tent o the warld
an aw its chynges.

Thir's naebodie leevin
wha really kens fir shair
whit we wir pit here fir, though
a wheen o fowk hae gey queer thochts.
Ower the years
we've seen some pawky sichts,
had a lauch or twae whan veesitors
sclam up thon brae.

A creeshie wummin
goat here, pechin, in a lang bleck ootrig,
reed herr spuein:
haiverin aboot 'vibes'
siller roon her airms
bangles an beads an whigmaleeries
aw aboot her.

Och, we've seen it aw,
hippies wi their luve-ins,
self-appointet mystics.
Halloween's fair hoachin wi
wutches an warlocks,
shair they ken whit's whit.

Bit years syne a bonnie lass cam
tae sit here wi her thochts an drames,
an whiles, she wis fair trachelt.
A ayeways thocht mebbe she kent
mair nor ithers whit we staun here fir.
Chrissie, fowk cried her, o Kinraddie.

Heart

Softer stones eroded,
granite heart remains;
glacier honed, Cairnsmore
stands proud, presiding
over emptiness.

Secrets of lives lie here,
buried beneath our feet;
dreams once dreamed
amongst silk-soft cotton
and wild orchids.

Only a rickle o banes
remains of Little Cullendoch.
Scattered on the hill,
sheep buchts and hay rees,
lonely reminders.

Defeat acknowledged
after years of struggle,
the people left.
Without haste, wilderness
obliterates their presence.

Lost in translation

Once, people spoke their maps.
Everyone knew where lay
rough moorland of the perilous region,
the hill of the eagle,
mountain of awesome grandeur.

Once, people were wary of the *crag*
of the storm-swept range, made pilgrimage to
the hill of the memorial pile or that other,
above the hollow of the warrior's tomb.

Once, people spoke their land
and what it meant to them,
before strangers, with inflexible tongues,
bringing pen and parchment, plotted

names which whisper only an echo
of what they once were:
Palgowan, Benyellery, Mulwharchar,
Craigmasheenie, Pinbreck,
Corrafeckloch.

Mither-tung

Learnin a new langage sno easy
when yir forty-seevin year aul,
Ma readin o it isnae bad, tho
A suspect A move ma lips
like a wean when A'm readin tae masel.

See screivin – a hale new ba gemm –
unlearnin whit ye didnae ken
ye'd lernt i the furst place, an noo
it turns oot it wis aw wrang onywye.

A've tae mind no tae pit an apostrophe
tae let folk ken a letter's missed
fir noo, the apostrophe's superfluous –
naehin's missin efter aw.

But ye still hae tae wunner if 'have'
is hae oar hiv oar huv. An is 'dark'
derk oar daurk? Ah'll hae tae mak the
deceesion soon, an choose which yin/wan is ma
mither-tung fir scrievin in.

At Carstairs Station

the waiting room was icy; passengers
stamped the platform's length:
the blue-skied sun sparkled frost.

A crow straggled past, flight path erratic,
made lopsided by the dead weight
of pigeon, carried in its beak.

It stalled, dropped between two tracks,
set about pecking, plucking its catch.
Little white feathers fluttered –

miniature snow storm. A second crow
joined the feast. Two magpies tried,
were chased away by angry caws.

Only one other passenger watched.
our eyes met – we looked away.
The blue-skied sun sparkled frost.

Ramshorn Kirkyard

The dead draw us in, entice the living
to consider past lives, wander
amongst quiet graves, where
headstones moulder, crumble to dust.

Ashes to ashes – appropriate here
where tobacco barons paid
to be laid to rest, their riches
opening heaven's gate.

Men traded cotton, tea, tobacco,
grew rich on the backs of slaves,
founded banks, entered politics
made this city what it is.

A smart topcoat of glamour and glitz
conceals now, as then, layers of poverty,
hopelessness and hunger,
the lie that wealth trickles down.

The voices of the poor are not heard here,
the entry fee to 'Paradise'* out of reach
for all but the wealthiest, who praised
their God each Sunday.

The dead draw us in, entice the living
to consider past lives, wonder
why lessons from the past,
are never learned.

**'Paradise' is the rectangular walled section within the graveyard. Richer merchants paid extra to be buried there.*

Hidden city haiku

secret hopeless place
spray paint graffiti artists
a silent story

rubbish spewing out
dereliction all around
our hidden city

Glasgow is changing
developers want it all
breathing spaces gone

Thousands pass here every day

don't notice this hidden place,
its crumbling, graffiti-ed walls,
windows boarded, bricked up
remaining panes jagged scars,

rubbish rots, damp moss tendrils
creep over cracked concrete,
underfoot, broken bottles crunch,
left by Tommy G, Josh, Jade and

others, who come to drink,
have a laugh, a piss, a shag,
paint their names on the bricks
remind themselves they exist,

don't notice new greenery
seed itself, in city-soil-filled cracks
buddleia bushes thrive
bring butterflies in summer.

Held to ransom

The boys won't allow Catherine and me
out of the sea; threaten us
with a dead fish whose stink,
carried on the breeze,
shrivels us closer to each other.

Rooted ankle deep in waves and sand,
strange sea creatures in hand-knitted cardies.
Now the tide covers our calves
tickles our knees; hems of tartan skirts
cling cold to salt-reddened legs.

Tears spill warm over cold faces,
the boys at last take pity, but demand
a ransom. If we don't pay, we drown.
Already late for tea, we capitulate:
me a flash of knickers, she a kiss.

We dry our tears, run home, hope
no one asks what's wrong? We know
we mustn't tell.

the battered octagonal tin

amongst the buttons
shimmering mother-of-pearl
once fastened gran's wedding gown

tiny painted forget-me-nots
from a dress mother wore
before she met my dad

dull brass buttons from
an unknown uncle's greatcoat

a tiny pearl, like a baby's first tooth,
gleaming almost in my grasp
sinks to the bottom

deep digging

silver threepennies for Christmas puddings
old farthings, two
real gold collar studs,
round rubber buttons
from an ill-named liberty bodice

tangles of coloured cottons
from wooden reels that grandpa
turned into bobbin knitters

or tractors
which wobbled jerkily
on rubber bands and matchsticks
across the kitchen floor.

Grannie Gillies wus a carline

Whan A wus a bairn,
Grannie Gillies,
the cailleach, they cried her,
leeved jist twae doors alang.
We weans wur awfie feart o her,
an gaithert evidence agin her
tae pruive whit we aw kent –
Grannie Gillies wus a carline.

Fir a stairt, she leeved alane –
her man, ma mither telt me,
hid lang syne drooned at sea –
wis skellie-eened
forbye bein awfie nebbie.
If she wisnae at the door –
a man's baffies oan her feet –
she wis keekin oot the windae
takkin tent o aw we did.
An if ony ither pruif wis needed,
she haed fower whuskers,
oan her chin.

Whan feelin michty wicht
we daured yin anither
tae chap her door an run awey,
tho we kent fine weel wi jist yin luik
she cuild chynge us intae puddocks
or mak oor nebs grow lang as lang.
Maistly, though, if haudin by her hoose.
we hunkert doon
an crowlt ablow her windae.

Yin day, whan waitin fur ma da,
Grannie Gillies hirpled by.

Afore A'd time tae flee, she spiered,
'Are ye goin fur a hurl
in yir faither's new motor?'
Fear stoapt ma tung fae wurkin.
A jist noddit,
afore takkin tae ma heels.

Whan A keeked back she wis staunin,
lookin awfie sad, an aw alane.
A didnae richtly unnerstaun
jist whit a felt then.
Noo, a ken –
Black burnin shame.

Growing pains

The shed was my shop,
my house, sometimes my stable
an old kitchen table, upended, my coach,
pulled by a jet black stallion.

Once, on a journey,
we stopped to rest.
I fed him grass, pulled
from where it grew sweet and
long between shed and garage.

I patted him, talked softly
to my trusty steed. Sudden sound
of laughter, unkind, made me
start and look.

Behind the midden, a face,
carrot-topped, popped up grinning.
My private world invaded,
a vanished horse, and
I, hands full of grass,
beside an upturned kitchen table.

Mixed messages

In primary seven our gym teacher
took the girls aside for an
explanation of menstruation.
Just as well – my mother
hardly knew where to start.

Embarrassment, like a silent fart,
hung in the air when,
in a voice not hers, she said:
periods are a natural function,
no shame attached, nothing to
worry about.

I nodded, didn't tell her I
was desperate to start, to be
initiated into mysteries of
Dr White's, belts with loops,
was jealous of my best friend's
stomach cramps.

On holiday – in Fleetwood – I woke
to blood-soaked pyjamas. Dad
was dispatched, with a note,
to the chemist. My joy was
short-lived – for the rest of the week
my mother kept telling me
to sit like a lady,
knees together,
not mention to anyone
this *natural function,*
no shame attached.

Africa in the news

Driving to work, listening to the radio
Africa on the news, politicians arguing
causes of famine:
wars, debt, drought,
'colonial legacies', says one,
and I'm ten again,
pink bits still on school maps,
gagging on radiator-warmed milk, banana flavoured.
The straw, made soggy by my resisting lips,
stops the flow, I slip the bottle back,
file into class, fighting nausea.

Mr Nicholson, menacingly pacing between rows of desks,
demands to know whose inch of milk has not been drunk.
Confession brings his ruler, crack across my knuckles –
a lesson quickly learned,
owning up brings punishment and pain,
not absolution –
Don't I know thousands of children,
starving in Africa, would be glad of the milk
I selfishly refused to drink?

My ten-year old brain grapples, fails
to accept the logic, but self-preservation
prevents a smart answer
passing my lips.
Not meeting his stare, I nod my head, dumbly,
but wonder, switching off the radio,
if I'd feel less guilt
had I drunk that milk.

UDI was declared in my primary school dining hall

We were there, 11th November 1965;
both halves of primary seven
watching a schools' broadcast
in the dining hall,
where they kept the television,
high on a trolley
the janitor wheeled into position.

An interruption
to the scheduled programme
brought a newsflash.

I couldn't have found Rhodesia
on the globe,
had never heard of Ian Smith, nor UDI,
but seeing our teachers –

lip sticked Miss Blackett,
cat-walk glamorous;
steely-eyed Miss Patterson, who every Friday
unbent to read us a tale of Para Handy
or Wee MacGreegor –

their faces grave,
nod knowingly at each other
I understood something big
had happened in the world we shared;

and we were there
11th November 1965.

Changed days

Although the Headmaster
didn't usually agree
with belting girls,
he made an exception:
1962 it was, she remembers it well,
reading Lady Chatterley's Lover
concealed inside The Tempest.

Nowadays, on a shelf
in the school library;
uncensored,
the gamekeeper's antics
with Lady Jane
seem tame compared to
Clockwork Orange or Trainspotting.

Facts of life

One Saturday morning,
helping mum make the beds,
I learned everything
she thought I should know
about sex.

Between married people she said
it's special; before –
lips tightened, voice dropped
to a conspiratorial hiss –
it's dirty.

In silence we cornered blankets,
smoothed candlewick 'til,
perhaps feeling a need to clarify,
she added:

Don't you ever bring trouble
into this house, my girl. I
don't have to spell it out,
you know what I mean.

I unlocked my eyes from hers,
plumped a pillow, hoped her lesson
hadn't come too late.

Home baking

The tins were never empty –
Empire biscuits, Gypsy creams,
shortbread fingers, coconut dreams –
unexpected visitors
would never catch her out.
Fairy cakes feather-light,
wings in place with butter-cream,
chewy meringues
in an air-tight tin,
Nestlé's cream on the shelf, just waiting
to be whipped into shape
if anyone dropped in.

But they never did.

She demanded warning
of visitors calling,
needed time to conduct her assault
on invisible dust,
to hoover and polish, find the best cups.

And though guests complimented
her home baking skills
she remained discontented:
their praises never enough

Tyranny of the victim

She hoards her losses;
a friend's death, a lover leaving, dreams dying …
recording in her ledger
the pains she's gained –
reckoning them worth more
than any of mine, or yours.

She will not be loosened from her grief,
pulling it closer,
keeping her warm as she gathers the seeds
of imagined slights and insults,
nursing them in a garden of misery
nurturing grudges into full-bloomed feuds.

Conspeeracy

They telt me thare micht be
a wee bittie 'discomfort' tae stairt wi –
no a thoosan reid-hoat needles
jaggin intae ma nipple,
like he wantit bluid, no mulk.

They said A micht feel kinna weepie
in the furst few days –
greetin an bawlin ma heid aff
no kennin whit fir,
like ma hail faimlie haed jist dee'd.

Quite forgettin tae mention
A'd torter masel –
imaginin hoose fires, kidnappins,
Saddam Hussain gassin Kurdish weans,
till A kent A cuid kill
onieyin hairmin ma bairn.

A think thir a conspeeracy amang mithers
tae keep quate, gin it's ower late.

Glorious boy

She revels
in every moment
with her son

but says, *if we could've*
been screened
I would've terminated him

Now she can't imagine
doing that because
she knows him – her beautiful child.

When he was an embryo, though –
a few cells …

She smiles, gathers her *glorious boy*
in her arms,

do you think
I would have given
this disease to anyone? With
no hope of cure or treatment?

Water God

(To David)

Sun-gleam on wet bronze limbs,
seal sleek you slip
into the deepest pool.
From the rocks I watch,
afraid of your fearlessness,
breath held as brown water
closes over you.
Surfacing, you laugh,
a careless toss of your head
scattering miniature rainbows –
my water god of the Otter Pool.

Other children splash,
playing safe
in sun-warmed shallows.
Their mothers silently question
my carelessness of you.
They do not know
how deep the fear,
how powerless
the mother of a deity
who believes he's indestructible –
my water god of the Otter Pool.

Youth

the sort old ladies
cross the street to avoid:
grungy clothes, unwashed air,
wild, spiky hair

metal studs in ears, nose, tongue,
eyes unfocussed, glaikit,
head jerking to iPod sounds
no one else can hear

poking through ripped jeans
two bare knees
make him suddenly harmless,
vulnerable.

Surprises

Once, my mother surprised me.
Can't quite remember the date,
though I know it was the last year
they played for the Queenshill Cup
on Carlingwark Loch.
Winter of waking to frost ferns
inside the bedroom window,
dad lighting a paraffin lamp
to stop the bathroom pipes from freezing.
The loch froze, hard enough to support
curlers and their granite stones, skaters,
children sliding on ice made slicker still
and those who came for the novelty
of walking on water.
I was surprised when my mother
fastened on a pair of skates she'd borrowed
and glided away, a sudden stranger.

Years later, on a summer day in the park
I saw the same surprise in your eyes
when I walked on stilts.

Chicken soup

I tear open Tesco's
ready washed and chopped
to throw in a pot
with half a dozen chicken thighs,

sense my mother's
breath on my neck –
hear her tut-tutting
my laziness, the cost

am taken back to my '60s
Saturday morning task;
she scrapes while
I dice carrots and turnips

chicken carcass simmers,
steaming up the window
as I dodge mum's tongue,
sharper than any knife.

Remembering Papa

I don't want to recall
a ward, silence
punctured by squeaky shoes,
curtained whispers
and an old man – rubber tubes sprouting
from a wrinkled yellow face –
wanting a kiss.

I'd rather remember
marching along
my hand in his:
'Left right, left right
I had a good job and I left right',
our laughter
at my six-year old feet
sometimes missing the beat.

Throwing crusts
to swans as
raspberry sauce scribbles
on ice cream cones,
singing together
at the Seaside Mission
'My cup's full and running over.'

The Shows in winter
his 'oh jings!' on the Dipper,
visiting Santa's department store grotto,
Papa's eyes crinkling at some private joke
when we met him again
in the very next shop.

I don’t want to recall,
refusing his kiss,
the pain in his eyes.
The memories I’ll keep
are our marching feet,
keeping time to the beat.

Water's edge

The water's edge restaurant opens,
a heron adopting his stately pose
watchful, patient, ignoring
busy red-legged oystercatchers,
gulls and guillemots.

One, I can't identify,
search the holiday hut for a bird book,
phone my father who at once
recognises the description,
gives its name, as I knew he would.

I tell him about the stoat – or was it a weasel?
'black tipped tail?' he asks – 'it's a stoat' –
that ran along the boundary wall,
up onto the roof
drank from the rain-filled gutter,
beady eyes twinkling, nose twitching
under my astonished gaze.

Dad laughs, we say goodbye.
A premonition of future loss
constricts my throat –
who will I call when he's gone?

Losing dad

It's funny how my dad was once
much taller than I;
shrinking years have brought us closer,
almost level.

Despite his stoop, lines, loss of hair,
he still looks like dad: the man
who gave me names of birds, trees,
stood in our garden pointing out
the Pleiades, Pegasus, Orion's
three-studded belt;

who helped me gather wild flowers –
red campion, ragged robin, star of Bethlehem –
pressing them between heavy books
for school projects;
who didn't mind the lawn
littered with obstacles –
clothes horse, kitchen stools –
to his lawnmower's progress
while my horse and I jumped clear
at White City;
who came to support me on every school sports day;
thought it fine for a girl to climb trees,
never laughed at my dreams,
opened my eyes to the world,
taught me the meaning of friendship and fairness.

But somehow my dad is fading,
empty spaces inside his head though
his voice sounds the same,

as he asks,

for the fiftieth time tonight:
what did you do today?

Caring for the elderly

A four-voice monologue poem

THE CARER

She's all right, Mrs. P, doesn't cause any bother,
unlike some I could mention.
Alice, for example, now she's a pain, all day moaning
she's tired, trying to get back to her bed.
If we let her do that, they'd all be doing it.
We'd spend our days fetching and carrying for them.
Some are just doolally – we don't say that in front of them, of course
–
and they want watching or they do the daftest things.
Jimmy went awol yesterday - found him eating leftovers from the
bin.
And Walter, well … I try never to be alone with Walter.
I know he can't help it but just the same, if he does it one more time
I'll slap him, I will.
But Mrs. P, good as gold she is, just sits quiet in front of the
telly,
even when it's not turned on.

MRS P's DAUGHTER-IN-LAW

It's very well run, the best in the area.
God knows it costs enough,
but for his mother it couldn't be less than the best –
not that she'd notice where she is, poor soul.
I offered to have her here, with us, but he said no. Thank God.
She's like a child – won't be potty trained, and can't be left
alone.
Before we found the Home she set fire to her bed one night. Can't
imagine why she's still allowed to smoke at her age.

He's at work all day, it would all be down to me.
Our children are away at last and I have plans
to decorate the house, take a course or two –
I thought ceramics or design. I'm quite artistic.
I really don't know how I'd cope if…of course, I would.
She's my husband's mother after all.
I did say she could come to us.

MRS P's SON

It was a hard decision but
I suppose it's best.
Mother really couldn't manage on her own,
having the Fire Brigade out was the final straw.
I wish she could come to us but …
well, I know it wouldn't work. I worry.
But she seemed all right last week,
though it's hard to tell – she doesn't know us, doesn't speak.
Once when Jan (that's my wife) left the room
mother clutched my arm, fingers like a vice
and mumbled something I couldn't catch
- it sounded like 'take me home with you.'
But it couldn't have been that.
After all, she never liked my wife.

MRS. P

I don't like it here, it's not nice.
There's a lot of old people around,
Strangers.
I don't speak to them - like mother always warned me.
They don't seem to notice they're being ignored.
The young ones - always on at me, Mrs. P this, Mrs. P that!
Don't they know it is Patterson, with a double t?

Always asking if I need to pee, it's degrading.
One of them has a nasty tongue and another,
she pinches when I'm slow to move.
Sometimes they don't switch on the television,
Laughing, thinking I don't know. I shan't ask them,
I'll tell my son when he comes to take me home,
he'll sort them out.
Time goes so slowly here …
Why hasn't he come?

My new normal

Life after loss, they say
becomes a new normal – things
are never quite the same.
My new normal is
never again trying to prove
worthy of your approval.
It's not having to show you
I'm grown up and mature,
talking about pension plans,
provision for the future.
It's singing off key, clapping out of time
not caring what you think.

Rubbing the numbness
of my loss to pins and needles,
warmth and feeling return –
bringing guilt because in others' eyes
my new normal came too soon.

Gretel's dilemma

It was either
her or us, I know that:
you boiled in a cauldron
me, oven-baked. Time
for desperate measures.

And father's joy when,
we came home safe,
pockets full of pearls,
never to know again
the gnaw of hunger.

Any court would accept
it was self-defence
but still, in dreams, I hear
her awful screams
as she burned alive.

Heigh-ho

Don't talk to me about dwarves.
Seven years a prisoner –
cooking, cleaning,
mending clothes.
making up their pieces.

never allowed out,
and let's not even mention
other favours
expected of me.

Telling you,
that poisoned apple
was a relief.

Two sides to a story

Fairy tales give us stepmothers
such a bad name:
all those stories about our
wickedness,
treachery,
vanity,
greed,
murderous tendencies.

No chance to plead our case,
explain how it is
when daddy's little princess plays
on his feelings:
grief,
loss,
guilt at a too-hasty marriage,
forcing him to take sides.

Worse, when daddy dies, leaving
us to deal with a teenage monster,
sulky,
spoiled,
selfish
beautiful,
hysterically blaming her stepmother.

Not easy to stay sweet
in the face of all that,
especially knowing, when the brat
comes of age, she inherits the lot.
Driven to distraction, no wonder we try
the odd poisoned potion, a spell or two.

Iraq 2nd September 2005

All day, mini vans and coaches,
bearing re-usable coffins,
choked the road to Najaf.

Each few minutes empty coffins
left the cemetery, to return re-filled
with yet more bodies.

Still frantic relatives searched
in searing heat amid the stench of
rotting corpses.

A thousand pilgrims crushed,
suffocated or drowned, mourned
by thousands more.

No one knows if 'evil design'
or simple panic started the mad stampede
across a Baghdad bridge.

The PM's spokesman blamed 'chaos'.
Seeking to stress normal life's return,
he told the world:

Yesterday, Iraq hanged
three murderers – first executions
since Saddam's fall.

A soldier hears his words,
sees the smooth smile and wonders
'is this what it was for?'

In 2005, nearly 1,000 pilgrims were killed in a stampede on the Imams Bridge, heading towards Imam Moussa al-Kadhim's shrine, after rumours spread that a suicide bomber was walking among them.

Living with war: Afghanistan 1990

Either side of the valley
opposing groups of freedom fighters
command two mountain tops.
During daylight hours,
they rest behind rocky barricades,
plan night assaults,
their presence ignored in the village below.

Men follow the land's rhythms,
plough, plant or harvest wheat;
women milk goats, weave carpets
share gossip and laughter.
School boys wonder what use
spelling to a *mujahid**, while girls
learn to sew, keep house,
sing songs at weddings.

At evening's swift darkening,
families gather, bread baked,
stories told, doors closed,
one by one lamps doused.
Then, tracer bullets arc
across night sky.
Children fall asleep
to kalashnikovs' lullaby.

•

* *Mujahid – a freedom fighter*

No answer

Eleven years of fighting
against each other
came to an end,
opposing Commanders
shook hands, embraced, told their men
they were now as one – brothers united.

Only Zaffar stood apart,
demanding: 'If these men
are not the enemy
I was taught to hate, tell me
how I reconcile
killing so many of my brothers?'

His mother says he's never
been the same, always fretting
how it came to pass
he's now on the side of the other side.
Here, we'd label it post-traumatic stress,
there, they shrug, call it life.

Arms dealer

Hassan bought one,
sold it on.
With the profit, bought another.

The family shook their heads,
knowing in the old man's time
it wouldn't have happened –
opposed to brother killing brother
in a war he couldn't stop,
never allowing anyone,
son or grandson,
to carry arms.

With his money
he bought painkillers,
for those who ached all over,
carrying loads too heavy;
iron pills and folic acid
for women, pregnant ill nourished,
Penicillin, Ampicillin, Streptomycin,
vitamins, sutures for open wounds;
believing the end
justified the means.

Maqour, Afghanistan

In a dusty brown town
kohl-eyed men in turbans strut,
roses behind their ears,
Kalashnikovs on shoulders.
They greet friends – and enemies –
with hugs, kisses on both cheeks.

From a door lintel a man hangs:
his bloated, bullet-ridden body
sways in a dance grotesque, a lesson
to others tempted to turn traitor.

Too late, I look away, horror
imprinted for ever more –
and think of a mother,
her heart now in pieces.

Beard

(For Hussain)

He was Hazara –
couldn't grow a beard.

Sometimes, though,
when he took medicines
to patients coughing in far places,
a soft furze adorned his chin,
testimony to his fear.

It wasn't enough –
on his last trip
Taliban caught him,
shot him.

Sometimes

Sometimes when the phone rings
I hope it's for me:

imagine I'll hear long distance,
a familiar voice saying hello,
your ear-to-ear grin,
winging along wires overland,
underground
to find its echo in me.

But, because it's been too long,
because I've worried, fretted, wept,
imagined the worst
I'm sharper-voiced than intended.
I'm in Iran, you'll laugh,
in answer to my question,
or Pakistan, maybe Moscow,
which you call *Moss-cow*.

It's been so long since
Jawad's letter came,
trying to explain, meaningless phrases –
doing all we can, Red Cross searching,
trying jails, don't give up –
on the page one word,
Taliban
stands out, says it all.
He'll call if they hear more …

Sometimes when the phone rings
I hope it's not for me.

Loss

A shroud of cloud for the moon,
dark shadows creeping.
Scent of lavender – not the calm
of aromatherapy's oil in burners,
nor the fustiness of sachets hanging
forgotten in old ladies wardrobes,
but strong, sharp,
growing in great wild tangles
on your mountains.
It breaches my defences,
the rolling echo of your last goodbye
and the feel of it –
a boulder, black, heavy
pressing me down.

Asylum seeker

Whan ye left yer hamelan
tae come tae mines
whit drames did ye bring
alang wi an embroidert hankie,
yer wife's tears in ivverie stitch;
photies o yer weans –
smiles tryin tae hide sair sichts
nae bairn shuild ivver see –
an yer ain wechtie hert?

Did ye think ye'd fin folk
wha'd unnerstaun
hoo it is tae ayeways be feart
fae the tirran's lang reach,
wunnerin the day if ye'll see the morn?
Did ye drame o bein free
tae wurk fir yer siller,
sleep easy an quate?

Hoo did ye feel
walkin intae Dungavel?

Hazara Jat

I remember mountains, that made mine small,
tearing jagged holes in a too-blue sky.
Hoopoes, orange crests bright in the sun,
patrolling the village, seeking
an uncovered milk pail.
Tea tasting of smoke.
Rattle of pebbles in a tin can
calling children home at dusk:
litany of names, *Iqbal, Shahnaz, Chaman* …
Smell of cow-dung, goats and dust,
mingling with vetch and clover.
And the scent of a little white rose
that would break MacDiarmid's heart.

Cutting fodder in Afghanistan

Butterfly bright,
in riotous rose-patterned frocks,
hunkered down all afternoon,
amongst milk-white clover,
purple vetch and pink *shaftal* –
with its heady, sugar-almond scent –
three women, with careless rhythmic ease
slice swathes of fodder.

Voices drifting
on pollen-laden air
dissect their world's events –
will Miriam's baby be here for Eid?
the calf born last week,
crickets eating Moosa's wheat,
and who caused Basma to hide her smile,
yesterday at the well?

Sweat runs ignored
down dirt-streaked faces,
arms ache for rest
but no one stops till
heavy creels flow over.
Each helps the other hoist her load,
rise to her feet.
They move away spines straight, shoulders back –
reluctant queens –
heads forced high by leather straps.

Harvest

Men scythe golden wheat,
patient bullocks
round the threshing ground –
the hard-packed dirt circle
centres the village –
men lift riddles high
let wind take the chaff,
under a big-bellied harvest moon.

Naoor

Naoor – a stourie plain in Afghanistan,
ringed aboot wi faur distant bens.
An a gey strynge bit it is,
whaur yir een play tricks
makkin muckle sma, an sma –
sic as sheep – big as hooses.
Thir a rax o blue watter, miles lang,
that isnae there at aw.

They telt me it's an optical illusion, but
A'm shair Naoor's warked oan
by an ill-hertit speerit.

A nivir seen sic poverty –
weans staunin by the road,
hurlin stanes at wur caur,
shilpit craiturs, bare-fuitit, faces chappt
by a snell wind bringin threat o snaw –
airlie September yet, hairst no ripe.
Temperature ablow freezin, we slept
happt i sleepin baugs an thermals,
unner a sky bleezin wi staurs.

In the mornin, efter dry breid an tea,
we saw weemin gaitherin wheat
stalk by stalk, as the furst snaw fell.

Mulberries in winter

Nimble-footed boys,
high in the branches,
made it rain ripe berries.

Flat mud rooftops
became patchwork quilts of
wine red, purple, black, white,

'til it was golden apricots turn
to lie in the sun, become *kishta*
for winter breakfasts.

Served with tea in glasses
dried mulberries in winter,
sweet reminders of summer.

Kishta – stewed dried apricots, often served with yoghurt.

Education

They laughed at me sometimes,
the women. Not unkindly
but with amusement
and bemusement as they unpicked,
yet again, my crooked stitches.
Or when I took my turn at spinning
the stone that turned the matted fleece
into wool, they'd smile behind their hands
at the fankle I
invariably made.
When I admitted that
I couldn't milk a goat
nor turn my hand to churning butter
they shook their heads and said,
'we thought in your country
women were educated.'

Taking turns

Sheep, goats, two small boys
helter-skelter down a mountainside
in a cloud of dust.

Smoke rises
from evening cooking fires,
hunger urges the boys homeward.

Tomorrow, it'll be their turn
to go to school, sit on tatty *gillims*
barely covering the mud floor,
alphabet chanting by rote;
alaf, bay, pay.

Learning in English class, 'O' is for orange –
not quite believing in a fruit they've never seen,
while their brothers guide flocks
ever higher,
searching for sparse pastures.

Buzkashi

Rearing, wheeling, plunging,
urged by leather-booted heels –
a rugby scrum of horses.
Whips and hooves, knife sharp,
slice frozen winter air as rising dust
meets sweat and steaming breath.
Laws of gravity ignored, a horseman leans,
crazy-angled, reins between clenched teeth,
and grabs the goat.

Men and animals scream defiance,
the maelstrom melts, dissolves –
a tidal wave of horses.
Thundering hooves become
thudding heartbeats, spectators roar approval,
ancestral memories stirred
by sounds and scents of victory.
No longer taxi drivers, labourers, shopkeepers,
they are Genghis Khan's army streaming –
invincible – across Asia's plains.

Tomorrow, the sound and the fury gone,
they'll be shopkeepers again.

Buzkashi – literally, 'goat-grabbing' – is an equestrian sport played with the carcass of a headless goat in Afghanistan and throughout Central Asia. It is said that in the original version prisoners of war were used.

Learning to walk again from experts in taking the first step

A land mine blew away his left leg,
and, in the gloom of the men's ward,
Farid struggles,
stumbles on a new prosthesis.
Leading him through the exercise
the physiotherapist by his side
moves with grace and precision
on his artificial leg.

In this hospital,
where eighty five per cent of staff
are amputees, the sharp odour
of hot melting plastic seeps from ovens.
Men, missing an eye, a hand, a limb,
mould new arms and legs,
fashion rubber from Russian tanks
into orthopaedic shoes.

The man in charge
watches lads with missing legs or feet
learn to walk. They lurch over concrete,
up a stairway, across a stretch of mud,
worst of all, a path of stones and pebbles.
Therapists on prostheses
catch them when they fall
and send them on,
up and back and round and up and back again.

Farid stops to rest,
the floor littered with artificial limbs,
abandoned where patients dropped them
to warm their stumps at a kerosene stove.
On mini-crutches two-year-old Sara Gul,
wearing a red dress, takes tiny steps on polio-withered legs.
The man in charge says, "this is not a sad place,
this is where new life begins."

Poem title taken from an article in LA Times 10/03/02 about an Afghan rehabilitation centre – a 'found poem'.

Thirteen ways of looking at a burqa

(after Wallace Stevens)

Burqa-clad women:
shapeless, formless, faceless,
uniform sameness.

The burqa is a topic
which obsesses,
polarises views – what's it to you?

Worn through choice
a burqa makes a statement:
modesty, purity righteousness.

According to Robert Byron,
travelling his road to Oxiana,
a burqa is 'a calico beehive
with a window at the top.'

A blue bag, a sack,
a bag lady,
lady wearing a blue sack –
a burqa.

Wearing a burqa means
no worries, ever,
about bad hair days.

A burqa's like a thief
who sneaks in the night,
steals women's identities.

An oven, a sweat factory
when temperatures rise
to forty degrees centigrade.

It's a grand disguise,
a way to hide
from people you don't want to see.

Worn by force, it's a
sky-blue prison, burqa abuse,
a shroud for women still living.

Men glance sideways,
wonder what a woman's wearing
underneath –

Lipstick wearing slick chick
hijab chic,
underneath her burqa
skin-tight jeans and tee-shirt

Its neat pleats obfuscate
issues of more importance
to Afghan women.

Smeddum

Whit they hud tae thole,
Afghan weemin,
doon-hauden, sair traitet.

Bit, dinnae think they taen it laen doon,
waitin fir a haun fae Bush's bombers.
Naw, they focht wi whit they hud,
douce, quate, happt in burquas,
ghaists flitterin saftly,

ayewise chancin
a baitin, jile, oar warse
tae bring buiks an learnin tae lasses.

Filmin a wumman pit tae death,
shot in a fitba stadium,
smugglin lipsticks
tae secret hooses,
mindin life
wis still wirth haein.

Word connections

Riffling pages of a Persian dictionary –
silently mouthing words, once spoken every day –
turns a key. A door creaks open
reveals heaps of rusty nouns,
adjectives, verbs for years unused,
stir into life.

They arrange themselves:
first, odd words, phrases,
then sentences group together form
snatches of conversations.
One of Aziza's jokes jumps up,
I push it back – never got the punch line first time round –

but here's Caca Qurban with tales of the land, of *djinn,*
fabulous monsters, locusts and snakes,
Jemila telling me how to cook *mantu* and *ash,*
Zahir confiding his love for Soraya –
words rekindle memories,
renew connections.

I hear myself in the clinic ask:
'*Nam chee'st*?'[1]
'*Chand sal asteed*?'[2]
a question often answered by a
universal shrug or,
'I was born the year the snows came early,
the year our wheat was lost.'
'*Taglif chee'st*?'[3] – the problem-probing question,
gave me more symptoms than I ever thought to know.

[1] *Nam chee'st – what is your name?*
[2] *Chand sal asteed? – how old are you?*
[3] *Taglif chee'st? – what is the problem?*

Seasons of fruit

Mulberries in July,
washed in snow-melt mountain streams
burst icily – sweet explosions on our tongues.

You laughed at my
surprise when the bowl you brought
in August held instead, golden globes of apricots.

I learned to play
your games of chance, winning kernels
to crack and share with you the sweet seeds inside.

Apricots gave way
to peaches, their fuzzy coats rough
on our tongues, sun-warmed melting flesh yielding.

Autumn brought walnuts, the sign to leave
before winter brought the snow.

Indigo Dreams Publishing
132, Hinckley Road
Stoney Stanton
Leicestershire
LE9 4LN
www.indigodreams.co.uk

Papers used by Indigo Dreams are recyclable products made from wood grown in sustainable forests following the guidance of the Forest Stewardship Council.